LLOYD LAING

LATER CELTIC ART
IN BRITAIN AND IRELAND

SHIRE ARCHAEOLOGY

Cover photograph
A detail of one of the terminals of the Tara brooch.
(By courtesy of the National Museum of Ireland.)

British Library Cataloguing in Publication Data: Laing, Lloyd
Later Celtic art in Britain and Ireland. – (Shire archaeology; 48).
1. Art, Celtic I. Title 709'.01'4 N5925
ISBN 0 85263 874 4

Prefatory note
This book mainly concerns itself with metalwork
and manuscripts. This is not because sculpture is
regarded as of less importance, but because it is
discussed in *Celtic Crosses of Britain and Ireland*
by Malcolm Seaborne in this series.

Published in 1997 by
SHIRE PUBLICATIONS LTD
Cromwell House, Church Street, Princes Risborough,
Buckinghamshire HP27 9AA, UK.

Series Editor: James Dyer

ISBN 0 85263 874 4

First published 1987; reprinted with amendments 1997.

Printed in Great Britain by
CIT Printing Services, Press Buildings,
Merlins Bridge, Haverfordwest, Pembrokeshire SA61 1XF.

Contents

Acknowledgements

I would like to thank Professor Barry Cunliffe and Dr Joseph Raftery for allowing me to use material from their excavations in the illustrations, and Dr Alan Lane for generously allowing me access to the material from his excavations at Dunadd. I owe a particular debt to Tasha Guest for drawing all the line illustrations, except figures 6, 7, 12, 19, and 22 and 23, which were by the author and figure 3 which was redrawn by D. R. Darton.

4

List of illustrations

1
The sources of later Celtic art

Between the fourth and twelfth centuries AD the early Christian Celts in Britain and Ireland evolved an artistic tradition of considerable magnificence. It has survived in metalwork, manuscripts and sculpture, with a few pieces in other materials such as bone and wood. The art is instantly recognisable for the unique way in which the components are juxtaposed: but it is paradoxically impossible to define. The more closely it is analysed, the less it tells a coherent story.

From the nineteenth century to the recent past early Christian Celtic art of the fourth to twelfth centuries was generally regarded as the last flourishing of a style that evolved in iron age Insular La Tène art. Recent research, however, has demonstrated that this view is simplistic. Whilst La Tène art is undoubtedly of the same genus as that of the early Christian Celts, the variety in vogue after the fourth century AD was markedly different.

The reasons for this must surely lie in the four centuries of Roman dominance in Britain. One reason for the original determination to see Celtic art of the iron age to medieval periods as a coherent whole was the lack of Roman material in Ireland, where, because there was no Roman 'interlude', the art had to be seen developing in a smooth run. Analysis and research into motifs and influences, however, show increasingly that the Roman contribution to Irish as well as British art was a formidable force. Roman artists made inroads into the Celtic mind and vice versa, where soldiers and politicians failed to penetrate. Art can thus be seen here to transcend human barriers as the essence of consciousness and truth. In consequence the study of Celtic art is not a mere cataloguing of motifs and items from museums, but of greater philosophical interest, a fact which is consciously and self-consciously acknowledged by those who admire and keep it alive today.

Celtic art of the early Christian period is probably best viewed in terms of a dynamic tradition constantly overlaid by new elements derived from outside. It typically utilises abstract, curvilinear elements. Yet these elements have a role, albeit minor, to play in Late Antique, Anglo-Saxon and Germanic artistic traditions. It is often very difficult to detect what is an essentially 'Celtic' end product: the Anglo-Saxons, for example, were capable of producing 'Celtic' designs in the fifth to eighth centuries as a result of their Romano-British inheritance.

Celtic art in Roman Britain, first to third centuries

Before the Roman conquest Celtic art (Insular La Tène art) was under the patronage of local chieftains. After AD 43, however, the patrons in Britain were no longer autonomous and therefore gained greater prestige in assuming Roman styles than in support for native flamboyance. Accordingly, in the first two centuries AD most of the products of Celtic art in Britain were relatively minor — items of enamelled horsegear, casket mounts and the like. In their design these often show a symmetry alien to the true products of La Tène tradition, as though the compositions have been balanced to appeal to Romanised masters. Nowhere is this more clearly seen than in the box mount from Elmswell, Humberside. This piece displays 'Celtic' lyre scrolls, berried rosettes (a feature of the latest manifestation of Insular art) and an enamelled panel of ivy leaves which look as though they have been copied from an Augustan silver cup or the rim of a samian bowl, which was probably indeed the case.

Caledonian metalwork

For the period centred on the second and third centuries AD some vestiges of a La Tène tradition can be detected in north Britain. In northern Scotland from the second century onwards a tradition flourished that has been labelled the 'Caledonian school'. Its most typical products are a series of massive bronze armlets and bracelets, such as that from Castle Newe, Grampian. On these, two important ingredients of later Celtic art appear, a confronted trumpet pattern and an enamelled stud (set into the terminals of the bracelets) with a chequer or cruciform pattern.

The same idea appears on a series of northern 'boss style' products, found mostly north of the Forth and dating from the

1. Enamelled bronze casket mount from Elmswell, Humberside; first or second century AD.

later second century AD. Of these the horsegear from Middlebie, Dumfries and Galloway, are good examples and also display another element of later Celtic art, the 'laurel-leaf scroll', which is clearly of Roman inspiration. There is reason to believe such works may have continued in production even into the fourth century AD, as is likely to have been the case with the less attractive products of the Caledonian school known as 'Donside' or 'massive' terrets. Such a late survival would account for the close relationship to the Caledonian school of a high-relief silver bossed plate from the Pictish Norrie's Law hoard (see figure 21), which was probably deposited in the early fifth century. This too has confronted trumpet patterns as an essential element in its design.

Irish Celtic art of the first to third centuries AD

In Ireland an art style can be distinguished which was contemporaneous with the Caledonian school. This is exemplified by the Cork horns, Petrie 'crown' and a series of relief-decorated discs, most notably from the river Bann and Monasterevin, County Kildare. Related in style is a mirror handle from Ballymoney, County Antrim. These pieces all use confronted trumpet patterns but have additional elements. The Ballymoney mirror handle has confronted beasts reminiscent of the animal heads on later hanging-bowl escutcheons, while the Bann disc and Petrie crown have as a common element a type of crested bird's head used as a terminal for a spiral. Once introduced, possibly out of Romano-British antecedents (for example on second-century 'dragonesque' fibulae) the crested bird's head recurs on a wide variety of objects. It was popular down to and including the early Christian period and can be seen on hanging-bowl escutcheons and hand pins. The Bann disc too uses a triskele pattern, which though La Tène in origin enjoyed a vogue in Roman Britain (see below).

These Irish pieces imply artistic links in the second to fourth centuries between Ireland and what later became Pictland and perhaps also hint at Romano-British influence on native art styles beyond the frontiers. Whatever the explanation, all the elements of dark age 'Celtic' style can be detected in Roman Britain, including those that have already been isolated here.

The main elements of Romano-Celtic art

A number of motifs appear in later Celtic art and are characteristic of it. They have other associations, however, and

2 *(Left)*. Mirror handle from Ballymoney, County Antrim; possibly second century AD.
3 *(Right)*. Key elements of later Celtic art: (a) pelta or palmette; (b) running scroll; (c) triskele; (d) yin-yang; (e) spherical triangle; (f) trumpet pattern; (g) confronted trumpet patterns; (h) ring-and-dot; (i) 'Durrow' or triskele spiral.

are not confined to use by Celtic artists. Of these the confronted trumpet patterns, triskeles, peltas, interlace and scrolls are the most prominent (figure 3).

Confronted trumpet patterns, typical of native art in Scotland and Ireland, are also, along with triskeles, to be found in a series of *trompetenmuster* ornaments scattered across the Roman Empire. These openwork horse-harness mounts have been found as far apart as South Shields (Tyne and Wear) and Dura-Europos in Syria. At Dura, and on the German frontier, they have been dated to a horizon of AD 165-256. Their travels have been explained in terms of troop movements. They were not exclusively Celtic, and indeed none of them may be of Celtic manufacture.

The triskele is a three-legged pattern with a variety of manifestations in Roman-British art. Its most notable appearance is on a series of disc brooches, dated to around the second to

4. *Trompetenmuster* ornaments: (left) South Shields, Tyne and Wear; (centre and right) Corbridge, Northumberland.

fourth centuries AD. Examples come from Silchester (Hampshire), Colchester, St Albans, Richborough (Kent) and also from the north. The Silchester brooch also displays confronted trumpet patterns. It has to be suspected that these and the *trompetenmuster* ornaments are the models for the Caledonian and Irish metalworkers, rather than the other way round. Simple triskeles also occur on a variety of other Romano-British objects, for instance on the base of a patera (saucepan) from Kingadle, Carmarthen, Dyfed.

Symmetrical non-zoomorphic interlace was also used in Roman Britain. The best examples are in mosaics, but a metalwork prototype can be found in the cable pattern which adorns one of the vessels from the late Roman hoard from Irchester, Northamptonshire. Romano-British mosaics also display double-strand interlace (a feature of Celtic design) as well as running scrolls, concentric circle patterns, swastikas and 'Greek key' or meander pattern. All these are apparent, for instance, on the famous Woodchester mosaic from Gloucestershire. Most of the remaining elements of dark age Celtic art also have their Romano-British antecedents. The curious design of crescent and circles that appears on the Barton, Cambridgeshire, hanging-bowl mount is matched on a strainer from the temple of Mithras in London. The pelta pattern that is so ubiquitous in later Celtic art can be found on a range of objects from fourth-century harness trappings from Richborough, Kent, and Leicester to inscriptions and seal-box lids.

5 *(Left)*. Romano-British brooch with triskele of trumpet patterns, possibly third century AD, from Silchester, Hampshire.
6 *(Right)*. Geometric interlace patterns: (left) four-strand; (centre) three-strand; (right) two-strand.

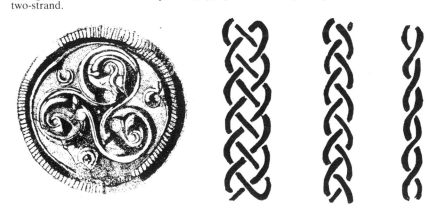

Ring-and-dot occurs on a variety of objects of both bone and metal from Lydney Park, Gloucestershire. Lydney provides virtually a pattern book for dark age art. The site was a late fourth-century shrine to the Celtic god Nodens, and the mosaics alone provide interlace, peltas, chequer patterns, concentric ornament, step patterns, spherical triangles, scrolls and star or marigold patterns produced by setting squares on squares. Lydney also provides some 'dark age' looking animals, rosette patterns, trellis ornament and complex hatching.

Object types

Almost all the metalwork that survives from the fifth and sixth centuries (and there are no corresponding manuscripts or sculptures that can be certainly dated to this period) exists as items of personal adornment, hanging bowls or their isolated mounts. As will be seen (chapter 4), the hanging-bowl series is firmly rooted in Roman Britain, and the hanging bowls themselves are a product of diverse workshops in both Celtic and Saxon areas in the pre-Viking age.

Of the personal items of decoration, the most important category is the penannular brooch. This has a respectable ancestry traceable back through Roman Britain to the Belgic iron age. In Roman Britain penannulars proliferated, especially in the north, where their later development should be sought.

In addition to these are various classes of pin, such as the hand pins, the development of which can be traced in north Britain again from the second century onwards.

There are a few decorated objects that do not fit these categories, notably mounts for caskets or horse harness.

Celtic Art and the traditions of migration period Europe

If later Celtic art evolved out of that of the Roman provinces, it nevertheless did not remain in a vacuum. There is strong evidence to show the influence of barbarian Germanic styles on the Celts.

One element apparent in dark age Celtic (and also Germanic) art is a type of naturalistic animal, executed with great economy of line. At its most characteristic the creature looks backwards over its shoulder or crouches, its legs folded under it. Its ancestry lies in the Eurasiatic traditions of the steppe lands of Russia and can be traced back to the Scythians and before. Such animals probably reached Europe during the upheavals of the migrations of the later fourth century. Mention has already been made of

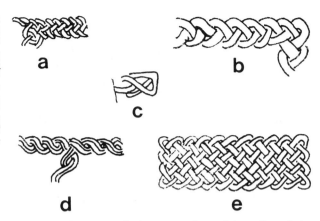

7. Romano-British interlace patterns: (a) mosaic, Brading, Isle of Wight; (b) mosaic, Eccles, Kent, about AD 65; (c) terminal of penannular brooch, Newstead, Borders, second century; (d) mosaic, Rudston, Humberside; (e) mosaic, Winterton, Humberside.

similar creatures from Lydney, and they are found in other late Romano-British contexts, for example at Wroxeter (Shropshire), Richborough (Kent) or Silchester (Hampshire).

In the mid fifth century they appear on a series of late Roman objects often found in Kentish cemeteries, decorated in what is known as the 'quoit brooch' style. Although from Saxon graves, the quoit brooches which give their name to the style have as their central element a penannular. The finest example, from Sarre, Kent, is also decorated with three-dimensional birds which can possibly be argued to be the forerunners of the bird heads on one of the Pictish 'Cadboll' brooches from Rogart, Highland. The strap mount from Croydon has a pair of S-shaped sea horses which not only hark back to one of the Lydney creatures but echo the similar animals on the openwork hanging-bowl escutcheons from Faversham, Kent, the creatures that form the hooks on hanging-bowl escutcheons, and the Pictish 'S-dragon' of later sculpture. In all these perhaps the Eurasiatic animal has been modified by Roman hippocamps but its ultimate ancestry is not in doubt.

In Anglo-Saxon England the Eurasiatic animal appears in various guises; on pot stamps of the sixth century from East

8. Quoit-brooch animals: (left) Alfriston, East Sussex, buckle plate; (centre) quoit brooch, Sarre, Kent; (right) quoit brooch, Howletts, Kent (all after Chadwick Hawkes).

Anglia; on silver coins of the eighth century known as sceattas; and even on some supposedly late Saxon disc brooches. In the Celtic realms the greatest manifestation of this animal art is on the Pictish Class I symbol stones, where the animals face forward but otherwise show the essential elements of the style.

The remaining repertoire of Celtic animal art is probably due to the influence of the Anglo-Saxon bestiary. In seventh-century England a fairly naturalistic creature evolved. This had a proclivity to bite itself and is in contrast to the disjointed animals found in the Anglo-Saxon Style I or the ribbon lacertines of Style II, which lack close counterparts in the Celtic world. In Anglo-Saxon England these biting beasts first appear around 625 in the Sutton Hoo deposit (on, for example, the shoulder clasps), and on a series of mounts from Caenby, Lincolnshire and a sword pommel from Crundale Down in the Isle of Wight. They may have reached the Celts via Northumbria in the second quarter of the seventh century — they are apparent in the Book of Durrow, and their descendants appear in Irish and Pictish metalwork. There are subtle differences, however, between them and their prototypes.

In Anglo-Saxon England can also be found the bird's head with hooked beak that appears in Irish metalwork, for example on the Tara brooch. In simpler form it appears on the terminals of a penannular brooch from Lagore, County Meath, and on brooch moulds from Dunadd, Strathclyde. These echo the heads on some Anglo-Saxon annular brooches.

These are but a few of the indicators that around the second quarter of the seventh century Celtic art was profoundly influenced by Anglo-Saxon traditions. To some extent the influence went two ways: in the seventh century a glass stud of Irish style was used to ornament a linked pin set from Roundway Down, Wiltshire, and foils decorated in Celtic style were inset into a mount from Swallowcliffe Down in the same county, to

9. Biting beasts from the Book of Durrow, seventh century.

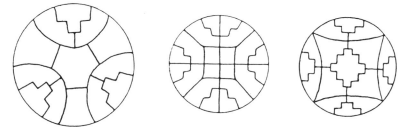

10. Anglo-Saxon and Irish boss patterns: (left) boss, Kingston brooch, Kent; (centre) glass stud, Moylough belt shrine; (right) roundel imitating a boss, Book of Durrow (all after Henry).

take but two examples. Nowhere is the interplay more apparent than in the enamelled studs of Celtic metalwork. Their ancestry, as has been suggested, may go back to 'boss style' metalwork of the Roman iron age in Scotland or to the similar bosses in Irish metalwork. Their designs with stepped and cruciform patterns must surely copy those on some of the Kentish disc brooches.

From the Anglo-Saxon world the Celts acquired many of the devices of the ornamental metalworker: granular and filigree work in gold (though these had been used in Romano-British jewellery too) and possibly pseudo chip-carving. Chip-carving, derived from woodworking, involves cutting inverse facets on the surface of the metal. It was a Germanic device, perhaps originating among the Goths at the head of the Black Sea: it is rare in Anglo-Saxon England. It appears in the fifth century on a number of early buckle plates and related pieces, probably of continental manufacture, and then again in Northumbria at a time when it was already fashionable among the Celts. Perhaps, then, the Celts adopted it directly from the continent — they were probably using it (for example on the Ardagh chalice) before it gained wide acceptance in Northumbria.

Of the remaining techniques employed by the Celtic smith, enamelling and millefiori work are both legacies from the Roman world. Both are extremely rare in Anglo-Saxon England, virtually the only enamelled objects of the pagan period being of minor note and mainly confined to East Anglia. The use of niello (a black paste formed from silver sulphide), though it occurs on pagan Saxon disc brooches, was similarly a Romano-British device, as was tinning or silver or gold plating, though they were also used by the Anglo-Saxons. True cloisonné work, so important in pagan Saxon jewellery, was seldom employed by the

Celts, and where it occurs, for example on a brooch from Croy, Highland, this may be due to a Saxon fragment being reused.

The remaining strand of influence on Celtic art before the Viking age was that of the Christian Mediterranean. Not very apparent in metalwork, though Celtic chalices seem inspired by Byzantine ones, this influence can be seen in both manuscripts and sculpture. The idea of the *codex* or bound book came from the Christian Mediterranean, and with it came an iconography of Mediterranean derivation. The evangelist portraits, the canon tables, the evangelist symbols and some of the decorative details of Celtic manuscripts are Late Antique, and so too are the models behind the iconography of many of the sculptures. Yet, as with all the other manifestations of alien traditions in Celtic art, the models were not slavishly copied, but subtly modified and altered, given local significance and blended into the organic whole of Celtic art.

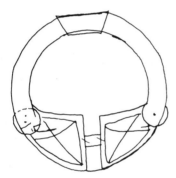

11. Designs from Irish motif pieces: (left) sketch for a penannular brooch, Nendrum, County Down; (above) grid laid out for design, Ballinderry Crannog, County Westmeath (both after O'Meadhra).

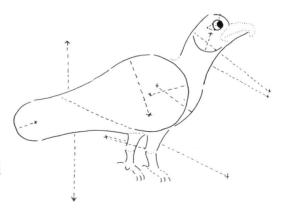

12. Eagle symbol of St John, Echternach Gospels, showing compass layout (after Henry).

2
The Celtic artist at work

As a result of the excavations of workshops and the discovery of unfinished pieces and sketches, as well as the finished products, it is now possible to study how the Celtic artist produced his masterpieces.

Almost every excavated site of the early Christian period in Ireland and Scotland has produced some evidence for metalworking. Frequently the debris from workshops includes moulds for some more ornate pieces. It may be assumed that as well as artist-craftsmen attached to the courts of Celtic chiefs or to monasteries there were itinerant smiths who travelled round the Irish Sea province making what was required and perhaps using their bags of scrap and samples as 'passports' across territorial boundaries. This would help to explain the eclectic character of later Celtic art.

In early Irish literature 'men of art' are accorded special status in society. It is likely that in the dark ages they enjoyed just such a status. This is suggested by the fact that sometimes the book illustrators or metalworkers 'signed' their works. They could be clerics or laymen attached to major ecclesiastical foundations.

Designing

The production of designs was not a matter of freehand sketching but was carefully controlled and laid out according to geometric rules. About 160 motif pieces (often called 'trial pieces') exist from Irish sites, and these show the draughtsman at work. They come from major monastic workshops (such as that at Nendrum, County Down), important royal sites (such as Lagore, County Meath) and even relatively minor ringforts (such as Garryduff, County Cork) and are usually pieces of bone or laminae of stone (slate was particularly favoured) on which a variety of patterns were tried out. Some may subsequently have been used for making moulds, wax impressions being taken from them. Others were preliminary sketches, of which not a few resemble the work of apprentices. This is the case with at least some of the large series of motif pieces from the 'Schoolroom' at Nendrum, which also produced the iron styli for drawing them and for writing on wax tablets.

The motif pieces show how grids were set out for rectilinear patterns and regular interlace, and how compasses were used to draw arcs of intersecting circles for the curvilinear patterns. This 'marking out' was also done in the case of finished manuscripts: tell-tale holes pierced by the point of compasses can be seen, for example, in the Book of Kells. In this manuscript areas of interlace infilled rectangular grids which were first lightly marked on the vellum. Spirals were produced by using semicircles drawn alternately from two centres, and more elaborate designs used a combination of grids, circles and arcs. Even animals, such as the eagle symbol of St John in the Book of Echternach, were produced in this way.

This technique was already being used in Ireland in the iron age, since compass-point marks are visible on the Lough Crew bone slips.

Mould making

Having worked out the design, the Celtic artist then turned to the production of moulds. Elaborate objects were produced by *cire perdue* (lost wax) casting, whereby a wax model was set in clay then heated to let the wax run out. This was done in the case of the elaborate crozier shrines, for instance: one from Hoddom, Dumfries and Galloway, was then finished off by turning on a lathe and engraving. Most simpler objects were produced by casting in bivalve (two-piece) moulds, which seem to have been used once and then discarded.

The design for the mould was set out normally on a die, which was impressed on the clay. A sophisticated lead die with a triskele pattern like those on some hanging-bowl escutcheons was found

13. Metalworker's equipment: (top left) triangular crucible; (top right) unfinished and broken casting of penannular brooch terminal, Clogher, County Tyrone; (bottom) tongs, Garranes, County Cork. Scales various.

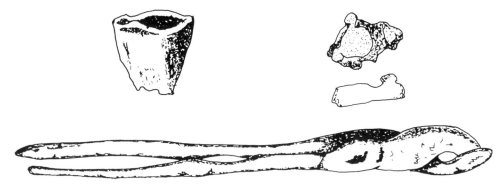

at Birsay in Orkney. This had a compass mark. For simple objects such as pins the die may have been made from bone and simply pressed into the clay: moulds, with the pins that were used as dies still fitting them, were found at Mote of Mark, Dumfries and Galloway, and Dunadd, Strathclyde. The moulds themselves have been found in large quantities (sometimes numbering several hundred fragments), notably at Mote of Mark, Dunadd and Birsay in Scotland.

At Birsay it was possible to establish exactly how the moulds had been made. Fine clay (sometimes mixed with sand for moulds without fine detail) was used to make the base pad, which was then given a rounded bevel to enable the second valve of the mould to be fitted over it. Piles of both sand and clay for mould making were found at Mote of Mark. The master pattern or die was then pressed into the mould and a preshaped *former* pressed in, to fashion the funnel-shaped ingate of the mould. A knife point was pressed into the clay round the edge, to allow for keying. The first half of the mould was allowed to dry in the air until hard enough for the second pad to be pressed down over the first. At this stage the top of the ingate was formed. When leather-hard, the die and the former were removed, and the join between the two mould halves was sealed with a strip of clay.

At Dunadd the moulds were sometimes pegged together with a small piece of wood. Keying was also done with a fingernail impression.

Casting

When the moulds were ready, metal was melted in a small, usually triangular crucible with or without a lid, in a charcoal furnace. Different types of crucibles were used for different metals. Heat was usually applied from above. The mould was set up at a slant in earth or sand, and the metal poured in. At Nendrum, County Down, the crucibles were set into stone holders, so that the tongs did not damage them as they were lifted from the heat, but at Mote of Mark, Dumfries and Galloway, one crucible has the impression of the serrated ends of the tongs indented in the molten residue on the crucible's side.

Sometimes several pins were cast in the same mould, being set fanwise. In other cases pins were pressed vertically into the mould and a wider ingate made for them. When cast, the pins were separated and the 'flash' removed.

The Celtic craftsman could vary his alloy according to his needs: at Mote of Mark both bronze and brass were produced.

Finished casts were sometimes silvered or more often tinned to make them look like silver. Silver objects were similarly sometimes parcel-gilt.

Techniques of ornamenting metalwork

Thin silver plates with relief decoration produced by repoussé hammering were sometimes made. This is known as *pressblech* and was a technique which originated on the continent, where it was used from the fourth century onwards in the making of helmets. In these cases a bronze, bone or iron die was used, and the metal hammered into it from behind. Dies for this kind of work are known from Anglo-Saxon England, though not from the Celtic world.

Very intricate knitted chainwork known as *Trichinopoly* was sometimes undertaken; it appears on the Derrynaflan paten (chapter 5), for instance. Special tools were probably required. When a modern craftsman was making a replica of a chain from the Pictish Gaulcross hoard a tool with prongs which fitted into a die had to be devised.

Filigree, twisted gold or silver wire, is often superior in the Celtic areas to the Anglo-Saxon. In Celtic metalwork the solder fastening the wires to the base plate seldom shows.

On the Ardagh chalice one thread of filigree was soldered on to another which was hammered into a notched ribbon. The notches can be seen on either side of the wire and gave the effect of sharp relief. On the Tara brooch ribbons of gold were set on edge to take beaded wires.

The glass bosses or studs that characterise the best Irish work were produced by putting a metal grille into a mould, pouring red enamel into some of the compartments, then filling the rest with blue glass, which thus gave both some outer blue cells and a blue core. The effect was subtle, translucent and variegated. Sometimes glass alone was used.

Enamelling was available in a variety of colours, though it is often now decayed and looks yellow where once it was red. From the later sixth or seventh century enamel may have been made from *cullet,* broken pieces of Germanic glass imported perhaps via Anglo-Saxon England. Champlevé enamel was the main type used, in which cells were cut away and filled with enamel, leaving the main pattern in reserve.

In Ireland *millefiori* work involved combining thin rods of coloured glass which were then stretched like sticks of 'rock' and sliced to be set (usually) in a sea of red enamel. Although

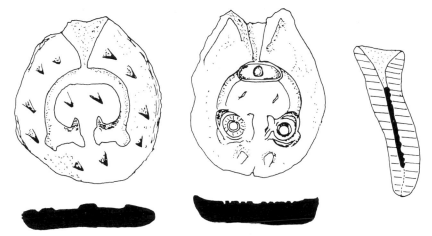

14. Front and back moulds for a penannular brooch and (right) reconstruction of casting method; Birsay, Orkney (after Curle).

millefiori was used on a few hanging-bowl escutcheons, it does not seem to have been a technique often employed in Britain but was introduced to Ireland perhaps from Roman Britain and remained popular until the Viking age.

Manuscripts

When the designs had been laid out, the manuscript illuminators appear to have produced both text and ornament as part of the same operation, for so integrated with the text were the decorated initials that it would have been difficult for the calligrapher to incorporate his text with the ornament. Goose and other quill pens were used for the script, and also for some of the ornament, though it is probable that brushes were also employed.

The pigments were a mixture of minerals and plant products. White or red lead, orpiment (yellow), verdigris (green), ultramarine (lapis lazuli, blue), folium (blue and pink to purple), woad (blue) and kermes (red) were all employed. Vinegar was added to the verdigris, which sometimes cut into the vellum. In the Book of Kells some colours were built up in layers: the ultramarine or verdigris was covered with a glaze of *folium rubeum;* ultramarine sometimes had a glaze of indigo; verdigris a thin layer of ultramarine. With this range of pigments the artist of the Lindisfarne Gospels was able deliberately to produce 45 pastel shades. Gold was not used (except for one initial in the Lindisfarne Gospels), gold effects being achieved with orpiment.

In the Book of Durrow there is no blue, but ox gall was used as a pigment.

Ultramarine was highly expensive, being produced from lapis lazuli, the provenance of which is unknown. In later periods it was brought from Afghanistan via the Arab world. The books were accordingly extremely costly to produce and highly prized.

Sculptures

A clue as to how the sculptor worked is provided by a number of unfinished works, including the Unfinished Cross at Kells, County Meath. Here the pattern was first sketched out (presumably painted) on the stone, then blocked out in rough relief. Next the background was deepened and the interlace executed. Then the head of the cross was begun and the figures were outlined. The detailed working of the figures was left until the end. Finished sculptures were almost certainly painted, as is known to have been the case with Viking age sculpture in England and Scandinavia.

Schools

By the seventh century the church had replaced kings and chiefs as the main patron of the arts. Manuscripts were undoubtedly produced in major *scriptoria* attached to monasteries. Celtic monasteries were the equivalent of towns, having communities of lay men and women attached to them.

Sculptures were probably produced by craftsmen operating from fixed, usually monastic, centres. It is possible to recognise groups of monuments of similar style round major foci. Local stone was used, and it is likely that the sculptors went out to execute their commissions rather than producing them in a central workshop. Kells, Clonmacnois, Iona, St David's, Maughold, Govan and Whithorn are but a few of the many foci for sculpture that are known.

3
Chronology

One of the most serious problems that besets the study of later Celtic art is that of dating. Virtually all the surviving works are without context or association and therefore have to be dated entirely on internal evidence. Thus many key works are dated on subjective opinion, and there is no actual evidence to suggest they could not be up to a century or more earlier or later than the date usually assigned to them. This subjective process tends to lead to circular arguments.

The outcome of this is that many major works have in the past been assigned to a wide variety of dates. The Moylough belt shrine, for example, has been variously dated between AD 700 and 850. So has the Ardagh chalice. The Pictish hoard of silver from Norrie's Law has been dated variously between 450 and 700.

There is a great deal of debate about the dating of 'early Christian period' sites in Scotland and Ireland. Some key sites were dated wrongly in the past through misinterpreted historical references, and this led to other sites being dated erroneously from them. There has been a tendency to start the 'early Christian period' at the meaningless but conventional point of the collapse of the Roman Empire, around AD 400. This date is not relevant for Celtic society, which was undergoing change from at least the second century. Many sites may have been occupied very much earlier than is assumed, and only a good series of radiocarbon dates (which are at present lacking) can rectify the balance. Some site dating is provided by imported Mediterranean pottery, but although some can be attributed to fairly narrow chronological horizons it is only applicable to the later fifth and earlier sixth centuries, a period at which there was comparatively little art.

Some works are dated through being associated with individuals or events. Some caution is necessary here, for can it be certain the association is genuine? The Cathach of St Columba is widely believed by many to be the work of the saint's hand and thus datable to the late sixth century, but it could quite easily be later. No one can be certain that the people whose names occasionally appear on works of art have been correctly identified. In any case, nearly all these 'dated' works belong to the later centuries of this survey, the dated metalwork belonging to a relatively short period between 1045 and 1127.

There are two chronological 'horizons' which can be helpful, if used with caution. The *Anglo-Saxon horizon* begins around the second quarter of the seventh century with the growing dependence of Celtic art on that of its Germanic neighbours. Thus it can be stated that Celtic objects which borrow techniques or motifs from the Anglo-Saxon are later than their prototypes. But by how much? There used to be a tendency to believe that there was a considerable time lag in the taking up of ideas by the Celts, but it seems unlikely for an Anglo-Saxon fashion to be adopted fifty years or more after it had fallen out of popularity with the Saxons.

The *Viking horizon* starts around the beginning of the ninth century. A series of pieces has been found in Viking-period graves in Scandinavia, and although some may have been very old when they were buried none can be any later than the date of the grave. Viking art styles, too, influenced Celtic art, and as these were subject to rapid development their period of influence on the Celtic world provides some kind of time limit.

A number of workshops found in excavation have produced moulds and in some cases castings. In the case of earlier excavations, it is not always possible to be certain whether the industrial activity belongs to one phase or more of the site on which they are found. Despite this, some general date brackets can be assigned to the workshops on the evidence of imported pottery or through being succeeded by datable occupation. These tentative date brackets are: Garranes, County Cork, about 450-650; Clogher, County Tyrone, about 475-600; Mote of Mark, Dumfries and Galloway, about 550-625; Clatchard's Craig, Fife, about 600-750; Dunadd, Strathclyde, about 600-850 (though some moulds may be earlier); Birsay, Orkney, about 700-850.

In addition to the material from workshops, there are a few hoards of associated objects, not necessarily all of the same date. The following are relevant: Tummel Bridge, Tayside, about 400-50 (though could be later); Norrie's Law, Fife, about 450 (some pieces may be older); Gaulcross, Grampian, about 450.

These are hoards of 'late Roman' type. A second group was deposited through fear of the Vikings or later: St Ninian's Isle, Shetland, about 800, though the hanging bowl may be earlier; Broch of Burgar, Orkney (lost), about 800?; Rogart, Highland, about 850; Croy, Highland, about 850; Ardagh, County Limerick, deposited about 950, but the chalice is much older; Derrynaflan, County Tipperary, tenth century, but the objects in the hoard are of the eighth to ninth centuries.

4
The Romanising phase of later Celtic art

As has already been argued, later Celtic art developed in Britain out of Roman traditions and thence was transmitted to Ireland. During the fifth and sixth centuries developments in Britain and Ireland seem to have run parallel to one another, with British craftsmen perhaps taking the lead. Early in the seventh century Anglo-Saxon influence made itself felt on Celtic art, and it seems to have declined in Britain outside northern Scotland. In Ireland, however, it came into its own, with new and exciting expressions. The later seventh and eighth centuries were the 'classic' period of Irish art, which was probably stimulated by interplay with Pictland via Dalriada. In Pictland art flourished in its own right.

Most of the material remaining from the fifth to mid seventh centuries comprises metalwork. The objects of the period up to 600 consist of hanging bowls or their detached escutcheons or basal discs, and various categories of dress fastener, along with a few isolated mounts.

Hanging bowls

There are about ninety known hanging bowls, either intact or as surviving mounts. A mystique has grown up round their origin, function and dating, most of it occasioned by a lack of understanding of the hybrid character of art in Britain in the late fourth to seventh centuries.

Hanging bowls are the direct descendants of a series of late Roman vessels, well exemplified by the hoard from Irchester, Northamptonshire, or the vessel from Finningley, South Yorkshire. Although they are mostly found in Anglo-Saxon contexts, they are the product of a lingering tradition of Romano-British art and were produced at various centres in Great Britain and Ireland. They fall into a number of distinct groups, of which the most notable are:

(1) Vessels with plain or 'heater' (shield-shaped) escutcheons; produced probably in southern Britain in the period 340-450 and later.

(2) Vessels with openwork pelta-pattern escutcheons: these are usually without enamel and may have been produced at several centres, including some in Pictland (there is a mould

for one from Craig Phadrig, Highland), the Midlands and possibly Ireland. Datable to 350-450 onwards.

(3) Vessels with enamelling and no openwork: these designs fall into a number of distinct groups, produced at various regional centres; they probably begin in the fifth or even late fourth century, but the majority seem to be products of the sixth.

The bowls probably served a variety of purposes and may have been suspended from a tripod, as the wearmarks on the suspension rings sometimes seem to indicate. Some may have had a liturgical function; some may have simply been for washing the hands. A few may have been used as lamps. One late example was certainly used for this purpose at Ballinderry Crannog in County Westmeath.

The fact that old escutcheons were reused on later bowls (for example at Badleybridge, Suffolk) and that single, stray escutcheons turn up in Anglo-Saxon graves suggests that they were treasured after the bowls had perished. Some were pierced for wearing and they have been found in contexts other than funerary, for example in the Saxon village of Chalton (Hampshire). They may have become regarded as symbols of *Romanitas* and possibly were used in gift exchange for status building in Anglo-Saxon England. This might explain some of the botched Anglo-Saxon attempts at copying them.

With the possible exception of a bowl from Chessel Down, Isle of Wight, which seems to have come from a sixth-century context, all the bowls from dated contexts were deposited in the seventh century, when many were already very old. In several instances they have been found containing food, such as nuts or crab apples.

15. Openwork hanging-bowl escutcheon from Hildersham, Cambridgeshire (left, side view; centre, front view), and enamelled basal disc from Crossthwaite Museum, Cumbria (right).

16. Hanging bowl with appliqué decorations; Lullingstone, Kent (reproduced by courtesy of the Trustees of the British Museum).

Penannular brooches

The most characteristic clothes fastener of the early Christian Celts was the penannular brooch. It was popular throughout the Roman period, and some types current in the Roman iron age continued to be used in the fifth and sixth centuries. Like the hanging bowls, the brooches have been the subject of considerable study, complicated by the fact that they were the product of a widespread folk tradition and were probably made in all parts of the Celtic world by itinerant smiths, who frequently experimented and produced hybrid forms.

One group of penannular brooches, the 'zoomorphic', is commonly regarded as 'dark age' but in their original forms the brooches of this group are probably of Romano-British manufacture. Along with other types of artefact, ornament and techniques, they were probably transmitted to Ireland in the late fourth or fifth century. There some brooches developed into distinctively Irish forms with enamel and sometimes millefiori on the terminals. These brooches have been well studied, and from the finds from Clogher, County Tyrone and the lead trial casting for one type from Dinas Powys, South Glamorgan, it is fairly certain that the Irish enamelled and millefiori versions were current in the sixth century and possibly in the late fifth.

A fascinating zoomorphic brooch with enamelled terminals of

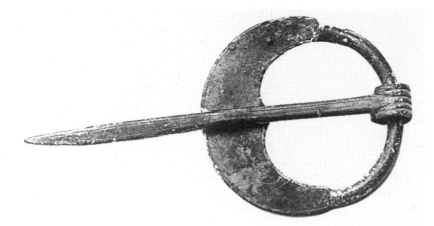

17. Bronze penannular brooch; Pant-y-Saer, Anglesey (by permission of the National Museum of Wales).

Irish form was discovered in excavations at Bath in 1978. One terminal has a bird (like a raven) grasping a fish (probably a salmon), the other a bird which is probably intended to represent a peacock. These are Christian symbols, current in the late Roman world, and the style of the animals is that of the Eurasiatic 'naturalistic' tradition. The associated material was late Roman, and the brooch is likely to have been lost sometime between the end of the Roman period and the battle of Dyrham in 577.

The same bird and fish motif appears on an appliqué on the hanging bowl from Lullingstone, Kent, in a similar style. The Lullingstone bowl also has naturalistic stags, with shoulder spirals, that recall Pictish beasts.

18. Terminals of an enamelled brooch from Bath, Avon (by courtesy of the Institute of Archaeology, Oxford; photograph by Bob Wilkins).

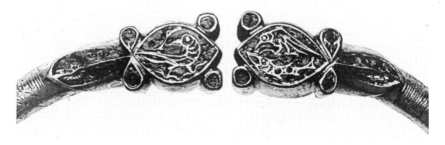

This period also saw the development of the penannular with flaring, flattened terminals. Despite claims to the contrary, there are no true brooches of this type in the Roman period, and they must be regarded as a development of the sixth and seventh centuries. Almost certainly they developed out of the zoomorphic form — their evolution can be traced in Ireland, in a series of zoomorphic brooches with increasingly flaring and flattened terminals. One of these reached Mull in Scotland, and their subsequent development is confined to Ireland and northern Scotland. One brooch, slightly more developed than that from Mull, was found at Pant-y-Saer in Anglesey, where it may have been taken by an Irish settler. Two rings from the Norrie's Law hoard have been claimed as penannulars of this type (see figure 21) but are more probably related to twisted torcs of the earlier iron age.

Brooches with flattened, round terminals are related. They constitute a separate tradition, but their development seems to run concurrently with that of brooches with triangular terminals. Their origins are difficult to determine but probably lie in late Roman Britain. They are more widespread than those with the flaring terminals.

Latchets and pins

Other forms of dress fastener are sometimes richly decorated. A peculiarly Irish form is the *latchet,* of which from outside Ireland a stray example comes from Icklingham, Suffolk, and the head of what may be one from Kiondroghad on the Isle of Man. They have serpentiform shanks, round which wire was coiled. Despite their mainly Irish provenance, they may originate in later Roman Britain (Icklingham is a well known late Roman site). The decoration of the heads, which includes a marigold pattern and a triskele of crested birds' heads, links them with the 'Romanising' hanging-bowl escutcheons.

One important type of pin was current in the post-Roman centuries. This is the *hand pin,* which clearly evolved during the Roman centuries in north Britain out of earlier types of projecting ring-headed pin. The real starting point came with proto hand pins, one of which was dated by association with a mid fourth-century coin hoard at Oldcroft, Gloucestershire.

True hand pins probably evolved by the end of the fourth or the early fifth century. Some have three and some five fingers, and the enamelled ornament may comprise either the motif that has been designated the 'hand pin eye peak' or a more sophisticated pattern such as occurs on the pins from the Pictish hoards from Norrie's Law and Gaulcross. There is a good series from Scotland, but most are Irish. They continued in vogue up to the coming of the Vikings.

The beginnings of Pictish silverwork

The beginnings of a rich tradition of Pictish metalworking can possibly be ascribed to the fifth and sixth centuries. The starting point can be seen in a hoard found at Norrie's Law in Fife, part of which at least is datable by associated Roman coins and scrap silver to the early fifth century. The objects in it include hand pins and two silver plates, versions of Roman plaques dedicated in shrines, which bear Pictish symbols.

To the same general horizon belong a variety of small objects which herald later developments and a series of massive silver chains, mostly discovered in southern Scotland, but in two cases with Pictish symbols on their terminal rings.

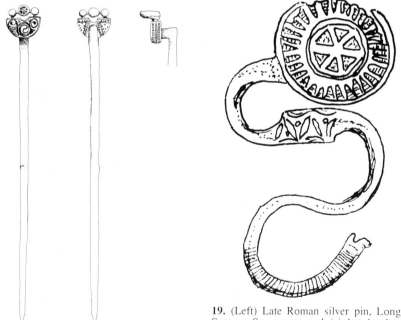

19. (Left) Late Roman silver pin, Long Sutton, Somerset, and (right) latchet brooch, Newry, County Down.

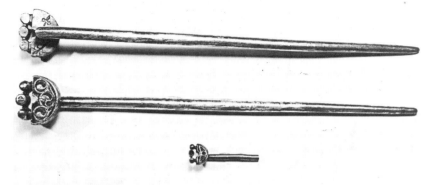

20. Hand pins, one with a Pictish symbol on the back of the head; Norrie's Law hoard, Fife (by courtesy of the Royal Museum of Scotland).

21. Part of the Norrie's Law hoard of Pictish silver (by courtesy of the Royal Museum of Scotland)

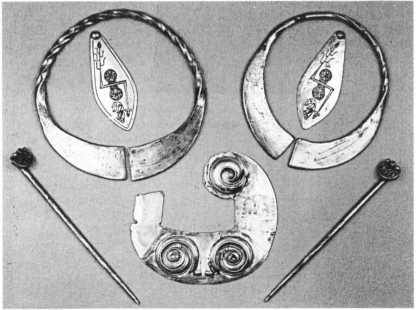

5
The golden age of Celtic art

The seventh century was an important period for Celtic art, since a truly Irish tradition evolved and insular Celtic art in Britain outside Pictland was eclipsed.

In the late sixth century non-zoomorphic interlace appeared in the Celtic world. The type that appears to be most characteristic had sharp angles and was multi-stranded. In Ireland it can be seen on a mould for a sword mount from Rathtinaun, Lough Gara, County Sligo, and in Scotland it appears on a series of moulds from Mote of Mark, Dumfries and Galloway, and on a sword pommel from Culbin Sands Grampian. This type of interlace contrasts with the zoomorphic Style II current in seventh-century England, but perhaps can be compared with that on a sixth-century sword pommel from Coombe, Kent, on some Saxon brooches and on a series of continental pieces. The tradition behind Celtic interlace may well be partly Romano-British – there is an example of multi-strand interlace on a penannular brooch from the Roman fort of Newstead, Borders – but possibly its adoption in late sixth-century Celtic Britain and Ireland was due to external stimulus from the continent, rather than Anglo-Saxon England.

Around the second quarter of the seventh century the techniques of granular and filigree work in gold reached the Celtic areas from Anglo-Saxon England. A fragment of a bracteate pendant from Tynron Doon, Dumfries and Galloway, shows the kind of model that was arriving, as do a gold and garnet harness pyramid from Dalmeny, Lothian, and a stud from Dunadd, Strathclyde. In Ireland the techniques were rapidly being used in an innovative manner on an intricate foil from Lagore, County Meath, and in a delightful and naturalistic bird from Garryduff, County Cork. In Pictland the earliest manifestation is on the terminal of an incomplete brooch from Croy, Highland, with a garnet inset, which can be taken along with the Dunbeath brooch from Highland (which is also Pictish) and the Hunterston brooch from Strathclyde as the first flowering of the Saxon-influenced style.

It has been shown that some techniques of Celtic filigree work are matched not in England but on the continent, in which case this may be seen as another source of influence.

The Croy and Dunbeath brooches were true penannulars,

22. Germanic interlace, before about 600: (a) from a brooch head, Freiweinheim, Germany, grave 10; (b) from a radiate brooch, Castel Trosino, Italy; (c) from a brooch, grave 56, Szentendre, Hungary; (d) from a disc brooch, Hockwold, Norfolk; (e) from a basal disc of a hanging bowl, Ipswich, Suffolk; (f) from a sword pommel, Coombe, Kent; (g) from a square-headed brooch, Ruskington, Lincolnshire; (h) from a square-headed brooch, Thornborough, North Yorkshire. (a-c after Haseloff, d-e after Scull, f after Davidson and Webster, g-h after Hinds).

decorated with fine gold wire. The slightly later Hunterston brooch and the Tara brooch (both probably Irish) are pseudo-penannulars, in that there is no gap between the terminals, which are joined into a plate. Pictish brooches seem to have always been true penannulars. The Croy brooch, although found in a much later hoard, could have been made as early as 650, and the Dunbeath brooch (which has an animal reminiscent of some Pictish creatures) somewhat later.

Far more sophisticated, the Hunterston brooch (found on a beach in 1830, having been at one time in the possession of a

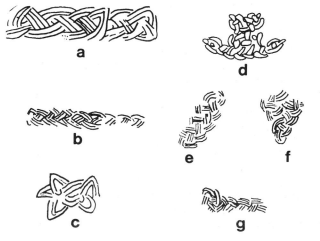

23. Celtic interlace, before about 625: (a-b) from a bone mould for a sword mount, Rathtinaun, Loch Gara, County Sligo; (c) from a sword pommel, Culbin Sands, Grampian; (d-g) from moulds, Mote of Mark, Dumfries and Galloway (a-b by courtesy of Dr J. Raftery).

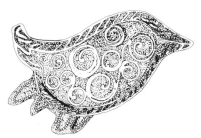

24. Gold filigree bird; Garryduff, County Cork (after Ó'Kelly).

Viking) is a masterpiece of the silversmith's art. As R. B. K. Stevenson has pointed out, if it was not made by a Saxon craftsman for Celtic taste, it was made by someone trained in a Saxon workshop. It is close in many of its details to some southern English products of the earlier seventh century. It can be compared with a buckle from Faversham, Kent, which has Style II filigree lacertine that is imitated, though not slavishly, on the Hunterston brooch. Because of details such as birds' heads that compare quite favourably with creatures in the Lindisfarne Gospels, a date around the end of the seventh century has been suggested for Hunterston, but it could equally well be a quarter of a century earlier.

To a slightly later date can be assigned the Westness brooch, from a Viking grave in Orkney. The filigree is not as fine, and it should probably be dated to the early eighth century. In both these brooches amber studs replace the garnet of Saxon work, as they do on the Dunbeath brooch. If the Dunbeath brooch is

25. Terminal of a silver penannular brooch with gold filigree decoration; Dunbeath, Highland (by courtesy of the Royal Museum of Scotland, Department of Archaeology).

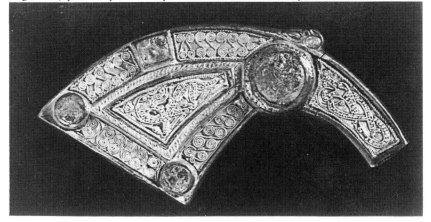

26. The Hunterston brooch, Strathclyde (by courtesy of the Royal Museum of Scotland, Department of Archaeology).

Pictish, those from Hunterston and Westness are possibly products of Dalriada, from where the idea of a joined terminal spread to Ireland.

Irish metalwork of the early to mid eighth century

The underlying problems of dating are illuminated in any discussion of the greatest masterpieces of Irish metalwork; the Tara brooch, Ardagh chalice, Moylough belt shrine and Derrynaflan hoard.

The *Moylough belt shrine* was found during peat cutting at Tubbercurry, Moylough, County Sligo, in 1943, without association. Designed to contain a leather belt (which was found to survive inside it), it has a skeuomorphic buckle and is made of four sections, hinged together. The ornament is extremely varied: champlevé enamel, millefiori, *pressblech* silver plates, coloured glass studs with metal grills, openwork plates and other devices are all employed. The motifs are equally varied, ranging from triskele patterns and peltas to trumpet patterns, birds' heads, animal heads and cells of L, T and S shapes containing enamel.

Many dates have been suggested for it (chapter 3). Those who favour a late eighth- or ninth-century date point out its similarities to some continental pieces of the period, such as the Adelhausen portable altar. Those who favour a date around 700 draw attention to features the buckle shares with late Roman/Saxon examples such as that from Mucking, Essex.

27. The Moylough belt shrine (by courtesy of the National Museum of Ireland).
28. Detail of the buckle of the Moylough belt shrine (by courtesy of the National Museum of Ireland).

The *Tara brooch*, which came not from Tara but from Bettystown, County Meath, is close stylistically to the Hunterston brooch, but arguably somewhat later. It is decorated with filigree 'Lindisfarne style' animals with long snouts (in simpler form they also appear on the Moylough belt shrine), glass studs with angular grilles (the patterns echoing the Anglo-Saxon tradition), engraved silver plates and relief ribbon animals with hatched bodies that appeared for the first time on the back of the Hunterston brooch. This type of animal with a double outline, sinuous body, flaring snout and hip or shoulder spiral is a dominant feature of eighth-century metalwork.

These beasts appear on a brooch from Mull (presumably a Pictish or Scottish product since it is a true penannular), on the silver hanging bowl from the St Ninian's Isle treasure (see below) and on a series of other items of metalwork usually assigned to the eighth century, such as the Steeple Bumpstead (Essex) boss. In England such creatures are absent, though their ancestors can perhaps be seen in a hybridisation of the Style II creatures of Sutton Hoo and the Lindisfarne animals.

On the *Ardagh chalice*, arguably the finest product of Celtic art, the fine filigree and granular work, the use of engraved silver, the bosses with their metal grilles, the enamels and inlays are all present. But there are new elements as well, notably chip-carving executed with great finesse on the stem. There are no Tara brooch animals here, nor millefiori, but instead the slender, trailing filigree echoes similar work done in Anglo-Saxon England, for the terminals now show plant-like features which are to be seen on the King's School, Canterbury, disc brooch, the Windsor sword pommel and the Kirkoswald trefoil brooch, all usually dated to the late ninth or early tenth century. Could the Ardagh chalice be as late? Its model certainly seems to be a Byzantine chalice, and its master craftsman seems to have been working in the mainstream of European traditions. Against this, however, the lettering on the bowl is distinctive, being found in Northumbria in the first half of the eighth century.

The Ardagh chalice and the small, plain chalice found with it (along with Viking brooches) were the only known examples of liturgical plate until 1980, when at *Derrynaflan,* County Tipperary, a cache of silver chalice, silver paten and stand, gilt bronze strainer and large bronze basin came to light on a major monastic site. The hoard was deposited in later Viking times, and the objects are of different dates. The chalice itself is crude compared

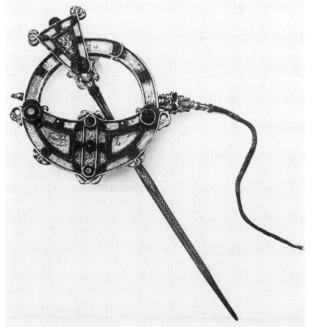

29. The Tara brooch. The length of the pin is 225 mm, or 9 inches (by courtesy of the National Museum of Ireland).

with that from Ardagh, and it is probably later, while the paten, stand and strainer belong with the Tara brooch and Ardagh chalice.

The earliest of the items may be the paten and stand, which bear gilded interlace patterns employing the same kind of strand as Sutton Hoo, done in *pressblech*, with panels of running scrolls and yin-yangs. At the top is trichinopoly wire work, in silver. The paten possibly dates from the late eighth century and the chalice can be no earlier.

The use of trichinopoly wirework (which was also employed on the 'safety chain' for the Tara brooch) raises the question of the date of the *Gaulcross* hoard of Pictish silver from Grampian. This has usually been assigned to the Viking period as it was felt the trichinopoly work could not be earlier. This obstacle removed, the Gaulcross hoard could be put back into at least the sixth century, bringing it closer in date to that from Norrie's Law.

Also probably Pictish is the *Monymusk reliquary*, a house-shaped shrine with enamelled strap grips and with mounts

30. The Ardagh chalice (by courtesy of the National Museum of Ireland).

31. The Derrynaflan chalice (by courtesy of the National Museum of Ireland).

decorated with chip-carved and enamelled ornament and with a pair of birds' heads on the gables. It is carved out of a block of wood, with attached plates, the front one of which is decorated with Pictish-style animals in light engraving. It dates from the eighth century and belongs to a group of similar house-shaped shrines, most of which are known from Scandinavian grave finds.

The St Ninian's Isle treasure

Discovered in 1958 under the chancel arch of a tiny church on a tidal island off the coast of the Shetland Mainland, the St Ninian's Isle treasure is the most splended hoard of Celtic metalwork yet discovered, the counterpart of Sutton Hoo. Buried around 800, the hoard comprises a collection of silver items, including the much older hanging bowl (see chapter 4), a series of silver bowls, a sword pommel, a pair of sword chapes with inscriptions in Irish lettering but with Pictish names and a series of penannular brooches. The style is distinctively Pictish and a series of related brooches has been found in many parts of Pictland, notably in another, mostly destroyed hoard deposited in the ninth century at

32. The Monymusk reliquary (by courtesy of the Royal Museum of Scotland).

Rogart in Highland. Animal heads are one of the elements in the designs, and similar but less accomplished brooches were being produced at Birsay in Orkney, as the moulds from the site reveal.

Manuscript art

Until the 1930s all manuscripts in 'Celtic' style tended to be ascribed to Ireland, and few doubted that the Book of Durrow or the Book of Kells were Irish products. Progressively, however, detailed study has suggested that relatively few of the surviving manuscripts of the 'golden age' were written and decorated in Ireland.

This is not to say, however, that there are no manuscripts of Irish origin, nor that no comparable works to the Book of Durrow or the Book of Kells were produced outside Britain. The earliest surviving 'native' (as opposed to imported) manuscript, the *Cathach of St Columba,* now in the Royal Irish Academy, would seem on balance of opinion to be a product of the late sixth or early seventh century, possibly executed by the saint himself.

It is a fragmentary volume, comprising 58 leaves of text with decorated initials (64 in all) done in red and brown ink. The

33. Three mounts, probably for a sword harness, St Ninian's Isle treasure, Shetland (by courtesy of the Royal Museum of Scotland, Department of Archaeology).

inspiration behind the initials was Mediterranean — such a device appears for instance in the *Vergilius Augusteus,* a fourth-century Italian manuscript — but in the Cathach they are integrated with the text. The ornament is simple and familiar: peltas, simple spirals, trumpet patterns, scrolls and curvilinear designs. The interest of the book lies in its position as the earliest known Celtic manuscript.

Celtic in style is another manuscript, produced at Bobbio, an Italian monastery founded by the Irish monk Columbanus in 614. This is the *Milan Orosius,* which has two confronted ornamental pages at its start, with a design of marigold patterns and cable interlace as well as chequer pattern. The initial letter has a stem which continues down the page, a feature of later Celtic and Hiberno-Saxon manuscripts, and red dots are used to outline letters, a device originating in Coptic Egypt.

After these tentative beginnings the story of manuscript decoration must be taken up in Britain. There is an important series of manuscripts that seem to have been produced either in Northumbria or under Northumbrian influence, as similarities in the palaeography suggest. The earliest is the *Durham Cathedral A II 10,* which probably belongs to the second quarter of the

34. Decorated initials from the Cathach of St Columba.

35. Carpet page from the Book of Durrow (by courtesy of Trinity College Library, Dublin).

seventh century. The decoration is still restrained, but there is more sophisticated interlace with knotwork and some animal lacertines with mouth lappets.

The *Book of Durrow* probably belongs to the second half of the seventh century, and current opinion suggests that it was produced on Iona in the monastery founded by the Irish St Columba. It is the earliest gospel book with a formalised arrangement of decoration, comprising whole-page decorative patterns ('carpet pages'), decorated initials and whole-page evangelist symbols. The treatment of the evangelist symbols is close stylistically to the animals of the Pictish symbol stones; the eagle symbol, however, looks like a Visigothic cloisonné brooch, and the man symbol, with his forward gaze and sideways walking feet, looks as though his robe is taken from a Romano-British mosaic. Most of the ornament in Durrow belongs to that of a Romano-British past, but some of the animals link up with the Crundale Down sword pommel and some of the interlace with Sutton Hoo, showing Northumbrian eclecticism.

Although an outstanding 'Hiberno-Saxon' manuscript, the

36. Chi-rho page, the Book of Kells (by courtesy of Trinity College Library, Dublin).

Lindisfarne Gospels need not be discussed here, as it is purely a product of a Northumbrian scriptorium, as is the badly preserved *Durham Cathedral A II 17*. The *Book of Echternach* has some Celtic features but was made at Echternach in Luxembourg. The *Lichfield Gospels* (Gospels of St Chad) is close stylistically to Echternach in some respects but is probably Northumbrian.

Although a product of the Irish-founded monastery at St Gall, Switzerland, the *St Gall Gospels* was made around 750 and is of great interest since it is stylistically a forerunner of the Book of Kells. It has a carpet page and the usual evangelist portraits (which replaced the symbols for the first time in the Lindisfarne Gospels) and also two pages depicting the Crucifixion and the Last Judgement. The colours are vibrant, the figures stylised into a pleasing linear pattern.

The *Book of Kells* remains the ultimate achievement of Celtic book illumination. Professor Julian Brown argued that it was almost certainly a product of a Pictish scriptorium of the middle to late eighth century, though one which was clearly influenced by the Northumbrian tradition. Current opinion is of the view that the Book of Kells was produced on Iona, probably in the late eighth century, on the occasion of the enshrinement of St Columba. The ornament is colourful, the arrangement masterly. Decorative work appears in carpet pages, ornamental text pages, portraits of Christ and the evangelists, miniatures depicting the Temptation of Christ, the Virgin and Child and the Betrayal, canon tables and decorative details. Influence in the design can be traced to several parts of the dark age world, yet the final product is distinctively 'Celtic'.

Sculpture

The only sculptures that possibly predate the seventh century are the Pictish symbol stones of what has been termed Class I – undressed stones with symbols incised on them. The symbol stones bear naturalistic animals and abstract motifs which are variously described as 'Z-rod', 'triple disc' and so on. The symbols also appear on some metalwork, cave walls and pieces of *art mobilier*. Long debates have surrounded their dating and interpretation: there is good reason to believe they developed in the fourth to fifth centuries in imitation of Roman tombstones and that they were primarily funerary. The abstract symbols, too, may have an origin in Romano-British art.

From the seventh century relief sculptures developed in Pictland, still with the symbols. These are usually combined with a Christian cross to produce a *cross slab*. By 800 the Picts were producing massive cross slabs covered with intricate detail (in some respects resembling the Book of Kells), such as the *Hilton of Cadboll* stone from Easter Ross, Highland.

In Wales there is little sculpture of note dating from before the Viking age, but in the Isle of Man there are a few works produced on the eve of the Viking settlement, such as the *Calf of Man Crucifixion* slab, which is an accomplished work of the eighth century.

In Ireland sculpture begins with cross slabs with some limited ornament, which may date from the end of the sixth or early seventh century. There then follows a series of cross slabs, both recumbent and upright, which span the duration of the early Christian period.

To the seventh century can be assigned the beginnings of figural ornament and relief work. By the end of the eighth century the characteristic Irish sculptural monument, the high cross, had emerged.

6
The Viking age and after

Although Celtic objects frequently turn up on Viking sites, where they are usually interpreted as loot, there are relatively few works of art that were produced during the Viking age.

One of the commonest groups of metal objects that are found in Viking contexts is mounts decorated with chip-carved patterns and interlace, sometimes with gilding or amber studs. These the Vikings tended to turn into brooches, such as one from the settlement at Jarlshof, Shetland. There are other mounts in similar style from Perthshire, Iona, the Isle of Man and England. In origin they seem to be Irish. Such objects were cast by *cire perdue* and not carved like their Germanic predecessors. To judge by the finds from Whitby, North Yorkshire, and elsewhere, a few similar pieces were perhaps made in Northumbria.

Also typical of the period are strap ends and related pieces engraved with rather weak interlace. Their models may be the 'Whitby' strap ends of ninth-century England: there are several examples from Scotland, including the Pictish Rogart hoard. They have been found in Viking graves in the Hebrides and the Isle of Man.

Scotland and Wales

From the arrival of the Norse there is growing evidence for the decline of art in Scotland. After the first half of the ninth century the Picts ceased to have autonomy, having been united with the Dalriadic Scots by Kenneth Macalpine. What sculpture there is north of the Forth-Clyde line is for the most part depressing. The monolith known as Sueno's Stone near Forres, Grampian, owes its battle scene and multiplicity of figures to earlier Pictish tradition. The Aldbar Stone, now in Brechin Cathedral, Tayside, is not without its charm.

In the field of manuscript art, the only product of note from Scotland is the *Book of Deer,* probably produced at or near Elgin, Grampian, in the tenth century. Even so, it is a poor thing, a distant cousin of the Irish 'pocket gospels' discussed below, perhaps put together through copying designs in the sketch book rather than an actual manuscript. The *Edinburgh Gospels* may also be a Scottish product but is not of great note.

Of metalwork the only noteworthy pieces are two croziers. The *Crozier of St Fillan* has interlace and running acanthus foliage; it

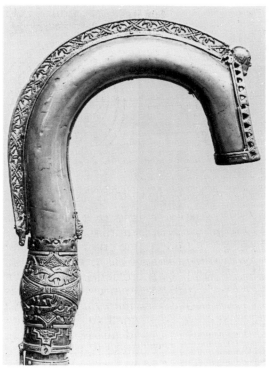

appears that surviving ornament could be a medieval copy of the late eleventh century. A second crozier from *Hoddom*, Dumfries and Galloway, is in cast bronze with animals that show stylistic affinities both to the Trewhiddle style of late Saxon art and its Irish counterpart seen on the Kells crozier. It dates from the early twelfth century.

In Wales there were several schools of sculpture in the Viking age and after, some of them quite accomplished, such as the Margam school and the Carew school. Apart from a few brooches, imports from Ireland and Pictland, there is virtually no metalwork. Manuscript art similarly languished.

It is therefore to Ireland that we must turn to trace the development of later Celtic art.

Metalwork in Ireland

The Viking raids and settlements brought about some changes in metalworking traditions. Enamelling generally fell out of favour, and filigree, where it was used, was coarse. While the traditional motifs still make an occasional appearance, they are largely replaced by foliage patterns of the kind that spread from

38. Animals from a knop of the Kells crozier (after MacDermott).

the Carolingian world to Anglo-Saxon England around the same time, and in which the acanthus reigned supreme.

The most notable works of the period are the group of croziers, the earliest of which, the *Prosperous Crozier,* has enamelling and dates from around 850. Three slightly later croziers may be taken together: the *Kells crozier* (or British Museum crozier, as it is sometimes called) and the *croziers of St Dympna and St Mel.* All have animal, plant or interlace patterns in small voids, after the manner of Trewhiddle-style metalwork, and all probably date from the late ninth century. Clearly, as these croziers show, chip-carved work was going out of favour by the tenth century, and filigree was similarly abandoned, though it came into favour again in the eleventh. In the words of Maire MacDermott (de Paor) 'Tenth century metalwork....has firmness and verve in the animal ornament and depends for its effect on the imaginative and skilful arrangements of the animal bodies and their lively and cheerful personality rather than an exquisite delicacy of embellishment pursued to infinite lengths.'

To the period around 1000 belong a few other pieces, such as the *Soiscél Molaise* and the *Clonmacnois Crucifixion plaque,* one of a group of such openwork mounts, which may have been used either on a book cover or a pax.

Metalwork of the eleventh and twelfth centuries

In the early eleventh century Irish metalworking revived. From around the end of the first quarter of that century the impact of Viking styles led to a renaissance of Celtic art, the old repertoire being reinforced by new Scandinavian animal styles. Some of these may originally have developed partly out of Irish impetus — the lip lappet is apparent on the beasts of the Kells crozier and it becomes an important element in later Scandinavian style.

Two Viking styles contributed to Irish art, Ringerike and then Urnes. The *Ringerike* style developed in the eleventh century out of the preceding Jellinge style. It is characterised by animal ornament with tendrils of acanthus-leaf foliage. The *Urnes* style, named after a wooden church in Norway, has highly elongated tendrils in which the plant origin is much less apparent. It continued to the mid twelfth century.

In this period in Ireland, as in England, silver became commoner, possibly on account of a new source in Viking plunder. A new device was the use of plait work of contrasting red (copper) and white (silver wire) hammered into grooves, giving a two-tone rope effect. This had been developed on the continent but was becoming unpopular there by the time it became fashionable in Ireland. A related technique involved the setting of silver ribbons in grooves cut into the bronze ground;

39. Head of the Lismore crozier (by courtesy of the National Museum of Ireland).
40. The Shrine of St Patrick's Bell (by courtesy of the National Museum of Ireland).

41. The Cross of Cong (by courtesy of the National Museum of Ireland).

these were usually bordered with niello, to give a black and white effect. The result has great impact and can be seen to full advantage on the Shrine of St Lachtin's Arm and the Clonmacnois crozier. It may be Byzantine in origin.

Of the older techniques, chip-carving and filigree revived, though the latter was coarse. Gilding was done by true plating.

A major centre for metalworking grew up round Kells in the mid eleventh century. Here the pure Viking Ringerike was soon replaced by an Irish variant with zoomorphic foliage, such as appears on the *Cumdach of the Cathach of St Columba.* This Irish Ringerike was succeeded by the Insular Urnes style. It can be seen at its best on the *Shrine of St Lachtin's Arm,* the Cross of Cong, and, in sculpture, on a sarcophagus in Cashel, County Tipperary.

There are a considerable number of important works belonging to the period 1025-1200. First there is a series of croziers, of which the *Innisfallen crozier* of the mid eleventh century serves as a bridge between the tenth-century group and the late eleventh-century *crozier of the Abbots of Clonmacnois* and the *Lismore crozier.* Of these the last is perhaps the most noteworthy, with its

42. Evangelist symbol from the Book of Dimma (by courtesy of Trinity College Library, Dublin).

degenerate Ringerike animals, lattice openwork and enamel settings, the studs echoing those of the classic period of Irish art. Urnes-style ornament also appears on the same work.

Of similar date, the *Shrine of St Patrick's Bell* was made to contain the still surviving iron bell believed to have belonged to the saint. It has elaborate filigree, added cabochon jewel settings and a crest with Urnes-style animals.

The *Shrine of St Lachtin's Arm* is inlaid with damascened patterns which cover all but the fingernails, the patterns being composed of Urnes-style animals with foliage.

The twelfth-century *Cross of Cong*, a processional cross which was made for a relic of the True Cross (covered by a piece of rock crystal and set in the crossing), is perhaps the finest achievement of Irish art in the twelfth century. It is covered with delicate, Urnes-style interlace, and at the base of the shaft there is an animal head which grips it in its jaws.

Irish manuscripts

After the time of the Book of Kells manuscript art declines, but there are a few important works. First, there is a series of 'pocket gospels', so called because of their diminutive size, which were undoubtedly produced in Ireland. They were often not bound but kept in a book satchel. They include the *Book of Dimma,* the *Book of Mulling* and the *Book of MacDurnan.* In all these the Chi-rho page (the opening of Matthew I,18) was important and elaborately decorated. The Book of Dimma and the Book of Mulling can be taken with the larger *Book of MacRegol* as a group of the eighth to earlier ninth century. The Book of MacDurnan has vivid colours and rich interlace and dates probably to the late ninth century.

Although no psalters of the ninth century survive, the tenth century is dominated by them. Notable are the *Cotton Psalter*, which dates from the early tenth century and is in a vigorous style, closely related to that of the Irish high crosses, and the *Southampton Psalter*, of the early eleventh century, which perhaps copied it. Unlike the former, it is well preserved (the Cotton Psalter was damaged in a fire in 1731) and has vivid colours. The *Psalter of Ricemarcus* (Ricemarch), now in Dublin, was produced in a Welsh scriptorium by a scribe who, though Welsh, had spent some time in Ireland.

The manuscripts described all belong to the period before 1070. For the period between 1070 and 1170 there are about twenty manuscripts surviving – evangeliaries, psalters, text books, collections of poems and epic tales in Latin and Irish.

43. The Psalter of Ricemarch (by courtesy of Trinity College Library, Dublin).

7
The legacy of Celtic art

The Norman conquest in 1170 brought to an end Celtic art in Ireland. The latest 'Celtic' manuscript in Ireland, *Cormac's Psalter,* was probably produced for a Cistercian monastery soon after the middle of the twelfth century. There is no Cistercian restraint in its decoration, however, for it is brightly coloured in blue, purple, green and yellow on red grounds, with ornate and complex interlacing initial letters and with charming little animal heads.

With the arrival of the Normans such manuscript art ceased abruptly and was succeeded by tedious copies of imported books. Much of the same happened to Irish sculpture, though now and again something of the Celtic spirit is discernible in the monotonous array of funerary figures. Metalwork survived a little longer: the *Breac Maodhóg* is a thirteenth-century shrine, its form copying an eighth-century predecessor. Although the work is mostly figural, there is some vestigial Celtic ornament, including chip-carving.

In Scotland no Celtic art outlived the Anglo-Norman penetration of the twelfth century, except in the west Highlands, where there was a tradition of grave slabs and a few free-standing crosses (such as MacLean's Cross on Iona), which carried an impoverished tradition through the middle ages and beyond. Elsewhere Celtic art was extinct — the *Kilmichael Glassary* and *Guthrie bell shrines* of the thirteenth and fourteenth centuries are in the tradition of dark age bell shrines but un-Celtic in taste.

In the sixteenth century there was a 'revival' of Celtic art in both Ireland and Scotland. The type of ornament that was favoured was interlace, and it may well be that the immediate inspiration came from renaissance Italy. This interlace can be seen in Scotland on the Eglinton and Fife caskets (sometimes dated to an earlier period) and on the Barr of Spottes flask, while in Ireland similar interlace can be found at the same period in sculpture and leatherwork, amongst other types of work.

In Wales no Celtic art outlived the arrival of the Normans, and there was no corresponding revival in the sixteenth century.

As boring and repetitive as that of the sixteenth century is the interlace that adorns powder horns made in north-east Scotland in the seventeenth century.

Persistant revivals led to a spate of 'Celtic art', particularly in

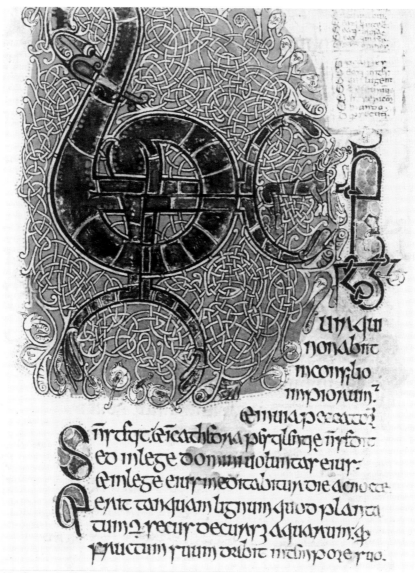

44. Cormac's Psalter (reproduced by permission of the British Library).

jewellery, in both Ireland and Scotland in the nineteenth and twentieth centuries. Twentieth-century Celtic art comprises either blundered patterns, heavily mixed with motifs of Viking origin, or slavish copies of ancient works of art. The term has become synonymous with weak interlace. It is symbolic of the past as wished for, a past in which the art, like the Celts that produced it, was wild and uninhibited. The reality is the opposite, for whatever else, Celtic art of the golden age was controlled and intellectual, the product of a disciplined reason, not an unfettered imagination.

8
Museums to visit

Intending visitors are advised to find out the times of opening before making a special journey.

British Library, Great Russell Street, London WC1B 3DG. Telephone: 0171-636 1544. The Lindisfarne Gospels is displayed.

British Museum, Great Russell Street, London WC1B 3DG. Telephone: 0171-636 1555. A representative collection of Celtic metalwork is on display, including a series of hanging bowls and penannular brooches from Britain and a good series of examples of Irish metalwork. Treasures include the Breadalbane brooch and the Kells crozier.

National Museum of Ireland, Kildare Street, Dublin 2. Telephone: (01) 677 7444. A magnificent display of all the treasures of Irish metalwork, including the Ardagh chalice, Tara brooch and Derrynaflan hoard.

National Museum of Wales – Main Building, Cathays Park, Cardiff CF1 3NP. Telephone: 01222 397951. All the few pieces of Celtic ornamental metalwork from Wales are on display.

Royal Museum of Scotland, Chambers Street, Edinburgh EH1 1JF. Telephone: 0131-225 7534. Virtually all the examples of Celtic art from Scotland are on display. Treasures include the Pictish silver hoards from Norrie's Law and St Ninian's Isle, the Hunterston brooch and the Monymusk reliquary.

Trinity College Library, Trinity College, Dublin. The Book of Kells and the Book of Durrow are displayed.

Ulster Museum, Botanic Gardens, Belfast BT9 5AB. Telephone: 01232 381251 or 381258. A good collection of metalwork from Northern Irish sites.

9
Further reading

There is no general survey of Celtic art in Britain and Ireland dealing exclusively with this period. Irish art is, however, well covered by the following works:

Bourke, C. (editor). *From the Isles of the North; Medieval Art in Ireland and Britain.* HMSO, 1995.

Henry, F. *Irish Art in the Early Christian Period, to AD 800.* Thames & Hudson, 1965.

Henry, F. *Irish Art During the Viking Invasions, 800-1020.* Thames & Hudson, 1967.

Henry, F. *Irish Art during the Romanesque Periods, 1020-1170.* Thames & Hudson, 1970.

Laing, L. and J. *Art of the Celts.* Thames & Hudson, 1992.

Laing, L. and J. *Celtic Britain and Ireland, Art and Society.* Herbert Press, 1995.

Mahr, A., and Raftery, J. *Christian Art in Ancient Ireland.* Two volumes: I, edited Mahr, Dublin, 1932; II edited Raftery, Stationery Office, Dublin 1941.

Ryan, M. (editor). *The Derrynaflan Hoard I: A Preliminary Account.* National Museum of Ireland, Dublin, 1983.

Ryan, M. (editor). *Treasures of Ireland.* National Museum of Ireland, Dublin, 1983.

Ryan, M. (editor). *Ireland and Insular Art, AD 500-1200.* Royal Irish Academy, Dublin, 1987.

Spearman, R. M., and Higgitt, J. *The Age of Migrating Ideas.* Alan Sutton, 1993.

Young, S. (editor). *The Work of Angels.* British Museum, 1989.

There is no comparable survey of art in Scotland in the period, but key studies are to be found in:

Henderson, I. *The Picts.* Thames & Hudson, 1967.

Small, A., Thomas, C., and Wilson, D. *St Ninian's Isle and Its Treasure.* Oxford for Aberdeen University Press, 1973.

Manuscripts are particularly well discussed in:

Nordenfalk, C. *Celtic and Anglo-Saxon Painting.* Chatto & Windus, 1977.

Also useful are:

Brown, P. *The Book of Kells.* Thames & Hudson, 1980.

Henderson, G. *From Durrow to Kells, the Insular Gospel Books.* Thames & Hudson, 1987.

Henry, F. *The Book of Kells.* Thames & Hudson, 1974.

56

Index

Page numbers in italic refer to illustrations.